MONTANA
a photographic journey

photography and text by
Stephen C. Hinch and Jason Savage

FARCOUNTRY
PRESS

Dedicated to my three nieces,
Trysten Nicole, Isabella Grace, and Elizabeth Marie.
—Stephen C. Hinch

I would like to dedicate my images in this book
to my wife Amanda and children, Owen & Maelle,
for all of your love and support.
—Jason Savage

Right: Completed in 1932 and one of America's most scenic drives, Going-to-the-Sun Road provides expansive views as it winds through Glacier National Park. Here, fall colors emerge on the park's west side. JASON SAVAGE

Title page: The sun rises over the Madison River near the town of West Yellowstone. The Madison provides important winter habitat for wildlife, and it's not uncommon to see tracks of moose, fox, elk, and other mammals, as well as waterfowl such as trumpeter swans, Canada geese, and an assortment of ducks. STEPHEN C. HINCH

Front cover: Swiftcurrent Creek flows into Lake Sherburne as the first light of the day reflects off Allen Mountain in Glacier National Park. JASON SAVAGE

Back cover: Elk graze on a hillside near Gardiner while Electric Peak looms in the background. At just under 11,000 feet, Electric Peak is the tallest mountain in the Gallatin Range of southern Montana. While it's still autumn where the elk are grazing, up on the high slopes, winter has already set in for the season. STEPHEN C. HINCH

ISBN: 978-1-56037-702-3

© 2018 by Farcountry Press

Photography © 2018 by Stephen C. Hinch and Jason Savage.
Text by Stephen C. Hinch and Jason Savage.

For more information about our books, write Farcountry Press, P.O. Box 5630, Helena, MT 59604; call (800) 821-3874; or visit www.farcountrypress.com.

 Produced and printed in the United States of America.

22 21 20 19 18   1 2 3 4 5 6

Left: Each spring mountain bluebirds, such as this handsome male perched on a barbed-wire fence in central Montana, return to the state, signaling warmer weather ahead. JASON SAVAGE

Far left: During a passing spring storm, a rainbow appears over a field of camas flowers on Priest Pass. Located near the town of Helena, Priest Pass, atop the Continental Divide, provides mountain vistas and large blooms of wildflowers each spring. JASON SAVAGE

Below: These gray mares, turned out to graze in the Custer-Gallatin National Forest, enjoy the warmth of spring amid green grasses and wildflowers in a mature stand of trees. STEPHEN C. HINCH

Above: One of the first flowers of spring, the pasque flower can be found throughout most of Montana. It's associated with Easter, hence its name. Pasque refers to the Passover, and the flower is also called the Easter flower. It has a natural "soft-focus" look due to the "hair" that grows on the petals. STEPHEN C. HINCH

Right: At over 11,000 acres, Makoshika State Park is the largest in Montana. The name comes from a variation of the Lakota word for "bad land" or "bad spirit," but there's nothing bad about this beautiful state park. Dinosaur fossils can be seen here among the badlands formations; please do not disturb them.
STEPHEN C. HINCH

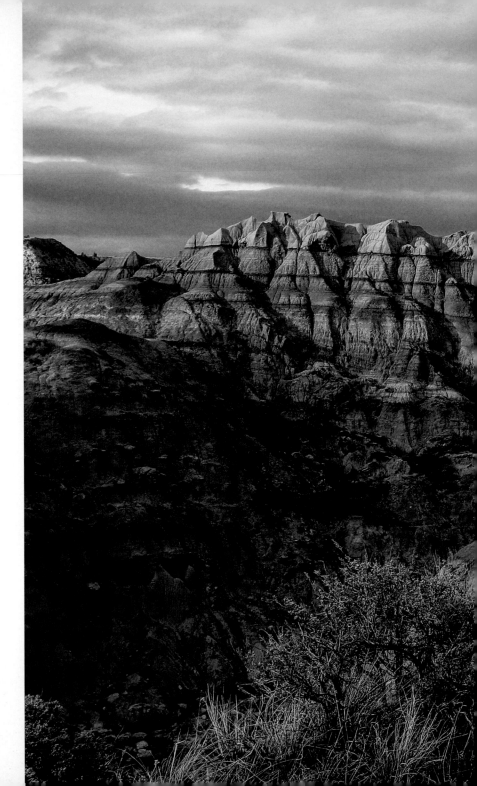

Left: A cowboy takes a break while working a cattle drive on a ranch in central Montana. JASON SAVAGE

Far left: As grasses start to green, snow still hangs on in the high country near the Smith River as cowboys move cattle across a ranch in early April. JASON SAVAGE

Below: Each July, the town of Three Forks hosts its annual rodeo, bringing in visitors from all around the state. During a break between events, a young cowboy gets in a quick nap on his horse.
JASON SAVAGE

This page: While Yellowstone National Park is largely in Wyoming, three of the five main entrances are located in Montana—at Gardiner, West Yellowstone, and Cooke City. The park was originally established to protect the incredible variety of geothermal features but today also serves as an important wildlife preserve, with grizzly bears, gray wolves, and bison among the park's inhabitants.

STEPHEN C. HINCH

Facing page: On April 24, 1903, President Theodore Roosevelt dedicated the arch at Yellowstone's north entrance near Gardiner. Today the north entrance is still the entrance of choice for many Yellowstone visitors, and the arch, which now bears Roosevelt's name, is a popular first photo stop.

STEPHEN C. HINCH

Above: Bald eagles can be found throughout Montana and are frequently seen around the state's rivers and lakes. Fish compose a large part of their diet, and it's not uncommon to see an eagle harassing an osprey to make it drop its catch. In winter, bald eagles hunt waterfowl. This eagle was perched in a tree above the Madison River looking for injured or ill mallards. STEPHEN C. HINCH

Left: The Absaroka Mountains rise high above the Yellowstone River as it flows through Paradise Valley, a beautiful valley north of Yellowstone National Park and south of Livingston. Large herds of elk and deer reside in the valley, while eagles and osprey perch in cottonwoods above the river. At sunset, when conditions are right, the clouds and mountains light up in a multitude of colors. STEPHEN C. HINCH

Right: At the head of Beehive Basin, above the town of Big Sky, a glacial cirque in the Lee Metcalf Wilderness is full of wildflowers in the summer. Montana is blessed with many such places high in the mountains, each one a treasure. Here the carpet of wildflowers is dominated by the abundant bloom of Indian paintbrush. STEPHEN C. HINCH

Below: During early spring on the Lee Metcalf National Wildlife Refuge, male wild turkeys put on a colorful display and strut their stuff, hoping to attract an interested female. JASON SAVAGE

This page: Each summer the Blackfeet Tribe holds its annual North American Indian Days, one of the largest gatherings of tribes from the United States and Canada. Dancers display their elaborate dress, colors, and dances during four days of celebration in Browning. JASON SAVAGE

Far left: Constructed by the Great Northern Railway just after the designation of Glacier National Park in 1910, Glacier Park Lodge at East Glacier is truly a sight to behold. Built with Douglas fir trees over forty feet tall and a three-story lobby over 200 feet wide, it remains a premier attraction for all to enjoy.

JASON SAVAGE

Right: A great gray owl perches on a branch as it waits patiently for its prey below. The great gray is not only the largest owl found in Montana but also, based on length, the largest in the world. They hunt rodents in meadows, where they occasionally can be seen by the patient and lucky observer. STEPHEN C. HINCH

Far right: The short hiking trail to beautiful Ousel Falls, near Big Sky, is both kid and dog friendly, and the falls are a popular destination on a hot summer day. Each season is different as the water levels vary. Spring runoff can make the falls run fast, creating clouds of mist. STEPHEN C. HINCH

Below: Early summer brings green grasses and wild irises to the foothills of the Rocky Mountain Front, where pronghorn and other wildlife are abundant. These pronghorn, or "antelope," as they are commonly called, take a curious look at the photographer before quickly departing across the plains. JASON SAVAGE

Above: In 1991, the U.S. Congress ordered the construction of an Indian memorial at the Little Bighorn Battlefield National Monument. The winning design, Peace Through Unity, was constructed near the park's visitor center and dedicated in 2003. "If this memorial is to serve its total purpose, it must not only be a tribute to the dead; it must contain a message for the living. . . power through unity . . ." —Enos Poor Bear, Sr., Oglala Lakota Elder STEPHEN C. HINCH

Right: Unlike the soldiers of the 7th Cavalry, who were buried where they fell, the Lakota and Cheyenne warriors were removed by their families and given traditional Native American burials. Beginning in 1999, red granite markers were added to sites where it was known that a Lakota or Cheyenne warrior fell. STEPHEN C. HINCH

Facing page, top: Last Stand Hill is the location where Lt. Col. George Armstrong Custer was defeated by Lakota and Cheyenne warriors in the Battle of the Little Bighorn in 1876. Today, a large monument sits atop the hill with the names of those who died. Many of the troopers of the 7th Cavalry are buried at the base of the monument, which was constructed in 1881. STEPHEN C. HINCH

Far right: The Custer National Cemetery is part of the Little Bighorn Battlefield National Monument. The cemetery was designated in 1886, although Custer had actually been reinterred at West Point nine years earlier. Veterans from other wars and eras are buried here alongside the men of the 7th Cavalry. STEPHEN C. HINCH

Right: The American kestrel is the smallest falcon found in the United States. About the size of a robin, they are commonly seen in fields and meadows as they hover in the air scanning for insects and small rodents. STEPHEN C. HINCH

Far right: Each spring, huge blooms of arrowleaf balsamroot blanket the hills surrounding the Rocky Mountain Front. Here, early morning light illuminates the Sawtooth Ridge on the Sun River Wildlife Management Area, with the wildflowers in full bloom. JASON SAVAGE

Below: Well known for its chain of many lakes surrounded by mountains, the Seeley-Swan Valley in western Montana draws visitors throughout the year to the calm waters of Seeley Lake. JASON SAVAGE

Right and far right: Virginia City is a well-preserved Old West gold mining town that appears much as it did during the peak of the gold rush. Founded when gold was discovered in Alder Gulch in 1863, the town is now largely owned by the state and is operated by the Montana Historic Commission. A photographer's dream destination, the old wood buildings provide great texture and character, and during the summer months, staff members in period costume add to the authenticity of one of Montana's most popular ghost towns. STEPHEN C. HINCH

Below: Nevada City, just a few miles down the road from Virginia City, is another Montana ghost town that was also settled during the gold rush of 1863. Today, visitors can stay in the restored Nevada City Hotel and Cabins. The town is an outdoor historical museum with several restored buildings that depict life in Nevada City during its gold rush heyday. STEPHEN C. HINCH

Above and left: Completed in 1902, Montana's Capitol is an example of the beautiful architecture constructed during the turn of the twentieth century in the West, and is a must-visit when touring Montana's capital city of Helena. JASON SAVAGE

Facing page, top left: Helena's outdoor "Walking Mall" hosts many iconic attractions, including the famous Bullwhacker statue that watches over downtown. JASON SAVAGE

Facing page, top right: Quickly constructed living quarters went up as mining boomed in Helena in the 1860s. Today, Reeder's Alley remains a well-preserved glimpse back into Helena's gold rush past. JASON SAVAGE

Facing page, bottom: Known for its profile resembling a slumbering man, the Sleeping Giant Mountain provides a backdrop to Helena's famous St. Helena Cathedral. JASON SAVAGE

Right: Bobcats are common throughout Montana, as they can live in a variety of habitat. Although bobcats are found from the plains to the mountains, it still takes a great deal of luck just to see, let alone photograph one. Their dappled tawny coats provide excellent camouflage in a landscape dominated by sagebrush and long grasses. STEPHEN C. HINCH

Far right: Cold temperatures and heavy snow blanket Electric Peak, near Yellowstone National Park's backcountry, seen here from a vantage near Gardiner. JASON SAVAGE

Below: Each year local mushers from around the region test their skills during the annual Darby Dog Derby at Lost Trail Pass. Here, on a frigid 20-below morning, a local Hamilton musher and her dogs compete with multiple teams during the first light of day. JASON SAVAGE

Above: Pompeys Pillar, near Worden, shows the only remaining physical evidence of the Lewis and Clark Expedition, with William Clark's signature etched into the rock alongside many Native American petroglyphs. Today, it's protected as a national monument. JASON SAVAGE

Left: Playful fox kits with their cute furry faces rank high on the list of great photo subjects for every wildlife photographer, although one should not get too close to the den site. This photo was taken with a long telephoto lens so as not to disturb the kits or their parents. STEPHEN C. HINCH

Far left: On their journey west in 1805, Lewis and Clark stopped at this section of the Missouri River, the confluence of the Marias and Missouri Rivers, unsure of which route to take. Lewis hiked up to the hill now known as Decision Point for a better view. He guessed that the clear waters of the Missouri must be from the high mountains in the west. The expedition voted and agreed with Lewis' decision, making a wise choice. JASON SAVAGE

Right: In 1895, just six years after Montana became a state, the bitterroot was designated as the state flower. One of the prettiest wildflowers, bitterroot blooms in late spring or early summer, depending on elevation. The Bitterroot Mountains, Bitterroot Valley, and Bitterroot River are all named after the wildflower. STEPHEN C. HINCH

Far right: The full moon rises over the Absaroka Mountains on a cold winter's night. Capturing a good full moon image requires a telephoto lens in order for the moon to appear large in the photo. Here, the peaks of the Absarokas provide the perfect frame. STEPHEN C. HINCH

Below: Lewis and Clark Caverns is not only one of Montana's finest state parks, it's also the state's first state park. Discovered in 1882, tours began in 1900, and it became a state park in 1941. Access is via guided tours that help to protect the delicate features and also provide interesting interpretive information for visitors. Each chamber has soft lighting, and the final chamber, called the Paradise Room, is lit with pink lights that are supposed to mimic what the formations would look like in daylight. STEPHEN C. HINCH

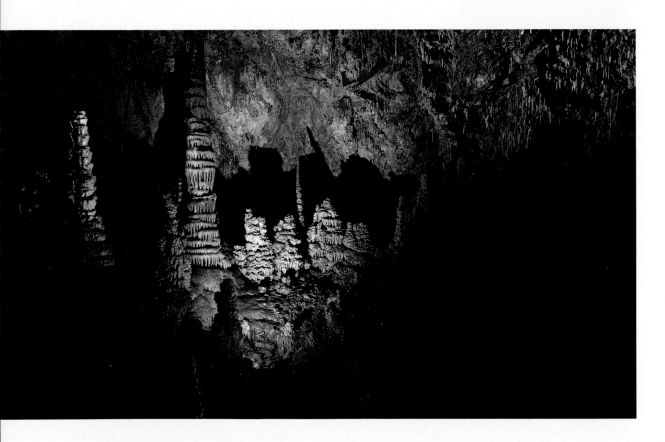

Above: Located on the North Fork of the Flathead River and just outside the most northwestern entrance to Glacier National Park, the famous Polebridge Mercantile is a popular stopover for hikers and visitors exploring the park. Known for its fresh-baked pastries, no visit is complete without a huckleberry bearclaw. JASON SAVAGE

Left: Moose are a common sight around Swiftcurrent Lake in Glacier National Park's Many Glacier area. Here, a bull moose wanders among the willows at Fishercap Lake during early fall. JASON SAVAGE

Far left: Chief Mountain, on the eastern edge of Glacier National Park, is just over 9,000 feet in elevation. Seen and named by Meriwether Lewis in 1805 as Tower Mountain, the name was changed in the nineteenth century to reflect the Blackfeet tribe's name for the mountain, Great Chief. The prominent peak is a popular photo subject, especially in autumn when the forest turns to gold. STEPHEN C. HINCH

Above: The bobcat mascot bronze adorns Alumni Square on the campus of Montana State University in Bozeman. Stately Montana Hall is located south of the square and has been one of the campus' central landmarks since 1896. STEPHEN C. HINCH

Right: Known for its historical small-town charm, Philipsburg is a popular destination during the summer months, bringing in visitors for local sapphire mining and its famous old-fashioned candy store, The Sweet Palace. JASON SAVAGE

Far right: A popular summer activity in Montana is whitewater rafting. Whether in a kayak or a raft, the waterways provide great recreational opportunities. The Gallatin River is popular for floating, and sometimes the river has flotillas of rafters coming through one after another—and why not? The scenery is stunning. STEPHEN C. HINCH

MUSEUM OF THE ROCKI

PLEASE
DO NOT CLIMB
ON BIG MIKE

Above: The Museum of the Rockies in Bozeman is a Smithsonian affiliate and a part of Montana State University. It is renowned for its extensive collection of dinosaur fossils; in fact, the *Jurassic Park* movies used the museum as a technical advisor. STEPHEN C. HINCH

Facing page, top: The Grizzly & Wolf Discovery Center in West Yellowstone is a wildlife park and educational facility that provides visitors an up-close view of grizzly bears and wolves. The animals seen here are rescue animals that would otherwise have been euthanized, and the center provides a unique opportunity to educate people about these species. STEPHEN C. HINCH

Facing page, bottom: The Beaverhead County Museum in downtown Dillon has been housing and displaying local history for over fifty years. Dillon was originally named in 1880 for Sidney Dillon, who at the time was president of the Union Pacific Railroad. The Union Pacific was building train tracks from Utah north to the mining areas of Montana, and Dillon, located in the Beaverhead Valley, made a natural choice for the creation of a town. STEPHEN C. HINCH

Above: On an early spring morning, a crane aggressively defends its nest against an unwelcome intruder. Each spring, small populations of sandhill cranes stop over to nest in wetlands throughout the state, with some paying a visit to the Lake Helena Wildlife Management Area just north of Helena. Just a few frames captured an amazing glimpse into crane behavior—and certainly a memorable moment for this photographer! JASON SAVAGE

Right: Sitting at just over 4,700 feet, Square Butte in Cascade County (not to be confused with the other Square Butte in Chouteau County) is a prominent landmark visible throughout the region just south of Great Falls. JASON SAVAGE

Below: In Crow mythology, Old Man Coyote created people, animals, and the earth. In some versions, Old Man Coyote is also a trickster, and that characteristic has remained part of the coyote's character. Trickster or not, the coyote relies on stealth to hunt, using all of its senses to locate prey. STEPHEN C. HINCH

Right: Each spring, greater sage-grouse gather on their mating grounds, called leks, in the grasslands of northern Montana. This male sage-grouse is putting on his elaborate mating display hoping to attract any potentially interested females. JASON SAVAGE

Far right: Dailey Lake sits beneath the imposing Emigrant Peak while sunset paints the sky and the peak in warm tones. The lake is a popular fishing destination, and a small campground sits on the lake's edge. A lucky camper might wake to the sounds of an elk bugling in September, or coyotes yipping as a trout breaks the water's surface. STEPHEN C. HINCH

Below: Elk can be found throughout the state, but there's no better time to see a big bull elk than in the fall. The bulls have shed the velvet from their antlers and are bulked up for the autumn rut, or breeding season. Cool, crisp mornings with the sound of a bull's bugle to break the silence, while autumn's golden grasses gently rustle in the breeze, is the ultimate Montana experience. STEPHEN C. HINCH

Left: Located in the Gates of the Mountains Wilderness on the banks of the Missouri River, the Mann Gulch Memorial remembers the thirteen smokejumpers who lost their lives battling the Mann Gulch Fire on August 5, 1949. JASON SAVAGE

Far left: Called Montana's "Most Historic City," Butte was once the mining capital of the world, boasting the largest population west of Chicago during the turn of the twentieth century. Today, it is home to a population of just over 30,000 and boasts a rich cultural history. JASON SAVAGE

Below: During the late 1800s, gold was discovered in the Garnet Mountains, prompting a building boom and the town of Garnet springing up seemingly overnight. Soon this small town had over 1,000 people and was a bustling little community tucked high away in the mountains of Montana. Today, Garnet Ghost Town provides a window into Montana's gold rush past. JASON SAVAGE

Right: Early October brings brilliant colors to the valley floor in the Bitterroot Valley. Near the town of Stevensville, a passing storm adds a touch of light and a rainbow to an already stunning scene. JASON SAVAGE

Below: Each fall during late October, the larch, or "tamaracks," as the locals call them, turn their brilliant golden hues and cover the Seeley-Swan Valley. A paddler on Rainy Lake glides through the reflections as the Swan Mountain Range looms overhead. JASON SAVAGE

Above: "In our family, there was no clear line between religion and fly fishing." So begins Norman Maclean's *A River Runs Through It*. In 1992, Robert Redford's film adaptation brought fly anglers far and wide to experience the romantic allure of Montana's Blackfoot River. JASON SAVAGE

Left: Mule deer are one of the most abundant mammals found across the state and can be seen in various habitats, from mountains to plains. In autumn, the bucks shed the velvet from their antlers as they prepare for the rut. STEPHEN C. HINCH

Far left: The Big Hole River makes its way through the Big Hole Valley, passing what remains of an early settlement just outside the town of Wisdom. JASON SAVAGE

Right: The prairie falcon, as its name suggests, is found in areas of open meadows and prairies, preferably with tall cliffs nearby for nesting. It is similar in size and appearance to its cousin the peregrine falcon, with which it is often misidentified. Like all falcons, the birds use speed when hunting their prey, which they try to catch by surprise by soaring in low and fast. STEPHEN C. HINCH

Far right: It must be summer when the beargrass finally blooms in Glacier National Park. This large wildflower often covers immense areas, making it a popular foreground for photographs with the rugged peaks behind. Not actually a grass, this beautiful flower is found in subalpine regions throughout the northern Rockies. STEPHEN C. HINCH

Below: In Glacier National Park, resident mountain goats greet hikers passing through on their way to Hidden Lake from Logan Pass on the Continental Divide—like this curious goat studying the photographer. JASON SAVAGE

Above: Any town that has a monument to a dog is a great place! Fort Benton, considered the birthplace of Montana, was founded in 1846 and was the first permanent settlement in the state. Behind the memorial to Shep is the Grand Union Hotel, which first opened in 1882. Shep's owner died in 1936, and his body was shipped back east by train. Shep spent the rest of his years faithfully waiting for the return of his master, never leaving the train station until he died six years later. STEPHEN C. HINCH

Left: The remains of an old building in a field provides for an interesting photograph. What purpose did it once serve? Was it a school or a church? A place that once served the people who lived nearby now slowly passes into time and out of memory. STEPHEN C. HINCH

Far left: The Missouri River is the longest river in the United States, approximately 120 miles longer than the Mississippi River. Its headwaters are in southwestern Montana, and it flows across the state through some of the most beautiful and rugged badlands and prairies. Popular for boating and fishing, the water of the Missouri is also essential to Montana's farmers. STEPHEN C. HINCH

Above: Founded in 1841 by a Jesuit priest, St. Mary's Mission is known for "Where Montana Began." The mission was built in a settlement initially called St. Mary's, which later became the present-day town of Stevensville.
JASON SAVAGE

Right: Home to around 350 head of bison, the National Bison Range at Moiese in western Montana was established by Theodore Roosevelt in 1908 and provides habitat for a wide variety of mammals and birds.
JASON SAVAGE

Far right: Native Americans used the high limestone cliffs at Madison Buffalo Jump State Park over 2,000 years ago. Herds of buffalo, or bison, were stampeded over the cliffs so they could be used for food, shelter, clothing, and other uses. Today the park protects this historic site, and the clifftops provide amazing views of the surrounding terrain.
STEPHEN C. HINCH

Left: Built around the turn of the twentieth century, the Bunkhouse Hotel adds character and charm to the small town of Jackson in the Big Hole Valley. JASON SAVAGE

Far left: Each spring, snow geese make their journey north to the Arctic, passing through central Montana for a stopover. During the last two weeks of March, thousands upon thousands of snow geese descend onto the ponds and fields at Freezout Lake Wildlife Management Area, located near the town of Fairfield. JASON SAVAGE

Below: Horses at the Triple Creek Ranch stay close on a cold December morning near the West Fork Bitterroot River. The West Fork area, southwest of the town of Darby, offers beautiful scenery and solitude. JASON SAVAGE

Above: Situated in the scenic landscape of western Montana, the University of Montana is located in Montana's second-largest city of Missoula. A bronze grizzly bear, the school's mascot, stands guard in the center of the U of M Oval. JASON SAVAGE

Right: A city landmark, A Carousel for Missoula, in Caras Park, displays its entirely hand-carved horses. The carousel opened in 1995, after four years and over 100,000 volunteer hours of work, and is a popular attraction in this downtown river park. JASON SAVAGE

Facing page: Showing off their roping skills, teams compete during Darby's annual Team Roping Rodeo, held each August in the southern Bitterroot town. JASON SAVAGE

Left: A nonnative to Montana, California quail were introduced in the not so distant past and now thrive in the western part of the state.. JASON SAVAGE

Far left: The Beartooth Highway is considered one of the most beautiful drives in the world. Starting in Cooke City, Montana, the road winds up through the mountains and crosses into Wyoming before dropping back down into Montana and the beautiful town of Red Lodge. The view from the top looks down into the heart of the Beartooth Mountains, a true Montana wilderness. STEPHEN C. HINCH

Below: The viewpoint at Devil's Canyon Overlook towers more than 1,000 feet above the water below in the Bighorn Canyon National Recreation Area, established in 1966. The point where Bighorn Canyon and Devil's Canyon come together is an incredible sight to behold. STEPHEN C. HINCH

Right: Trumpeter swans once were found over most of North America, but by the 1930s there were fewer than 100 of them south of Canada. Despite being the largest North American waterfowl, the trumpeter still has all the grace one would expect of a swan, especially when stretching its wings to catch the early morning light. STEPHEN C. HINCH

Far right: Red Rock Lake National Wildlife Refuge was created in 1935 to protect migratory waterfowl, including the trumpeter swan. Efforts at the refuge to save the swans were very successful, and today they are estimated to number around 46,000. The beautiful Centennial Mountains provide the backdrop for the refuge, which provides habitat not only for swans but also moose, bears, pronghorn, deer, and most other wildlife species found in the state. STEPHEN C. HINCH

Below: Almost one-quarter of the Pryor Mountain Wild Horse Range lies in the Bighorn Canyon National Recreation Area. The Wild Horse Range sits on the border between Montana and Wyoming and was established in 1968 to protect and provide habitat for the area's free-roaming wild mustangs. This beautiful stallion made his presence known to a young colt who had wandered away from the herd. STEPHEN C. HINCH

Right: Founded by Marcus Daly, one of Montana's copper kings, Anaconda is located in Deer Lodge County and sits in the foothills of the Pintlers, formally known as the Anaconda Range. The grand neoclassic-style county courthouse was constructed in 1898. JASON SAVAGE

Far right: Whitefish Lake, a short distance from downtown Whitefish, is a popular destination in the summer for swimmers, boaters, and water-skiers. Big Mountain of Whitefish Mountain Resort looms in the background. The ski resort becomes a summer playground during its off-season with scenic lift rides, mountain biking, and other activities. JASON SAVAGE

Below: Located in Great Falls and discovered in 1805 by Lewis and Clark, Giant Springs is one of the largest freshwater springs in the country and a popular destination for both locals and tourists visiting the area. JASON SAVAGE

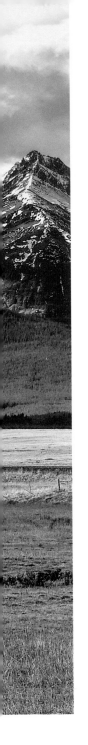

Left: Each Saturday, locals set up their booths at the downtown farmers market in Hamilton, making it a good place to find locally grown produce and other fresh eats. JASON SAVAGE

Far left: Trains and Montana go hand in hand, and many of the towns and cities throughout the state owe their beginnings to the rails. Today, trains still carry their loads across the plains and through the mountains just as they have since the state's early days. STEPHEN C. HINCH

Below: In most towns in Montana, it's not office towers that scrape the sky but grain silos. These three silos in Loma were photographed with a telephoto lens at sunrise from Decision Point. Rugged hills, cottonwood trees, and farming are all part of the way of life here. STEPHEN C. HINCH

Above: The sun sets behind mystical badland formations in Makoshika State Park near Glendive. Caprock Trail is a short but wonderful hike that takes visitors past incredible formations including hoodoos, caprocks, and other sandstone formations that shouldn't be missed. STEPHEN C. HINCH

Right: In the heat of summer, even this desert cottontail is smart enough to find a cool place out of the sun. While it might be cool in the mountains, out on the high plains the summer sun can heat things up, and wildlife must adapt to the seasonal changes. STEPHEN C. HINCH

Far right: One of Montana's most easterly state parks, located just outside the town of Glendive, Makoshika is an otherworldly landscape of ancient seabeds littered with fossils. JASON SAVAGE

Above: Local winter enthusiasts snowshoe through Lolo Pass' excellent network of cross-country ski trails near the Idaho border.
JASON SAVAGE

Left: The American marten, or pine marten, is a member of the weasel family and can weigh up to three pounds. Ghosts of the forest, they move silently as they hunt rodents and can be difficult to spot. In the winter, they're a little more visible against a snowy backdrop.
STEPHEN C. HINCH

Far left: A 1,200-acre wildlife refuge located in the Bitterroot Valley, the Teller Wildlife Refuge is home to the historic Slack Barn, highlighted here in a classic Montana winter scene. JASON SAVAGE

Above: The incredible views in Glacier National Park make for some of the best hiking in North America. The sun sets behind this hiker as she makes her way back to the trailhead after a day exploring Glacier's backcountry. STEPHEN C. HINCH

Right: A fly fisherman tests his skills on the Bitterroot River near Hamilton. The Bitterroot is a blue-ribbon trout fishery running eighty-four miles from the confluence of its west and east forks near Connor to its confluence with the Clark Fork River near Missoula. JASON SAVAGE

Far right: The view of St. Mary Lake with Wild Goose Island rising from its waters like some mystic wizard's fortress is one of the most iconic scenes in Montana. Regardless of the time of day, the view here is magical as the glacier-carved mountains drop thousands of feet to the lake below. At almost ten miles long, the lake is the second largest in Glacier National Park. STEPHEN C. HINCH

Left: Along the edge of the Missouri River in Fort Benton's Riverside Park is this monument depicting Meriwether Lewis, William Clark, Sacagawea, and her infant son, Pompey. The monument, by renowned western artist Bob Scriver, commemorates the nine days the Corp of Discovery spent camped upriver at the confluence of the Missouri and Marias Rivers. STEPHEN C. HINCH

Far left: Melita Island, located just off the shores of Flathead Lake, is uninhabited, undeveloped, and owned by the Boy Scouts of America. The sixty-four-acre island provides local habitat for wildlife and has been home to Boy Scout gatherings since the 1940s. JASON SAVAGE

Below: The boardwalk of Trail of the Cedars, one of the most visited locations on Glacier National Park's west side, winds its way through an ancient cedar grove near Avalanche Creek. JASON SAVAGE

Right: The western meadowlark is the state bird of Montana. In 1930, when schoolchildren were asked which bird best represented the state, they overwhelmingly agreed it was the western meadowlark. In 1931, the state legislature concurred and named it the state bird. One of the first harbingers of spring, the meadowlark's song always signifies the end of winter. STEPHEN C. HINCH

Far right: Founded in 1862, Bannack originally served as the capital of Montana Territory in 1864 before it was moved to Virginia City. Originally a mining town, eventually the population dwindled, with the last of the residents leaving in the 1970s. Located near the town of Dillon, today the ghost town is preserved as Bannack State Park, drawing thousands of visitors each year. JASON SAVAGE

Below: Each November during the bighorn sheep rut, echoes of crashing horns can be heard across the canyon walls as bighorn sheep rams test their strength in an amazing display of power and grit as they compete for dominance in the herd. JASON SAVAGE

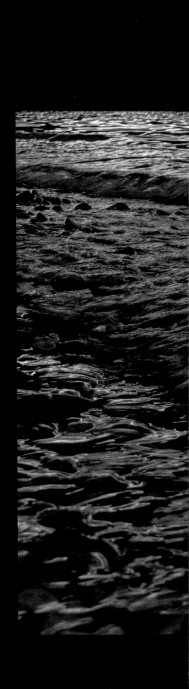

Above: Nestled under Lone Mountain in Big Sky, the Soldiers Chapel was established and dedicated in 1955 by the Story family as a World War II memorial. The nondenominational church is open to the public May through September with services on Sundays from Memorial Day to Labor Day. STEPHEN C. HINCH

Right: When alarmed, white-tailed deer erect their tails as they run off, causing the white underside to show. The mule deer has a rope-like tail and larger, mule-like ears. Both deer species can be found in the same habitat, and both are common on farmlands. This whitetail buck pauses for a moment at sunset before darting off across the meadow. STEPHEN C. HINCH

Far right: Wade Lake is a spring-fed lake in the Beaverhead National Forest. Once a well-kept secret, Wade Lake has become a popular destination, and also provides important nesting habitat for birds of prey including bald eagles and osprey, which are commonly seen.. STEPHEN C. HINCH

Next page: A long exposure displays the Earth's rotation through star trails above the Sleeping Giant Mountain near Helena. JASON SAVAGE

Stephen C. Hinch

Award-winning photographer Steve Hinch is a full-time resident in West Yellowstone. What was supposed to be one summer in Yellowstone has become more than a decade of living and working in the Yellowstone area.

Through his wildlife and landscape images from across the country, Hinch shares unique views of nature as they happened in that moment in time. Hinch's images have been featured in a variety of publications and collections, including the Smithsonian Institution National Museum of Natural History.

To see more of Steve Hinch's photography, visit www.stevehinchphotography.com.

Jason Savage

Based in Montana, Jason Savage works as a commercial photographer specializing in travel and outdoor photography. His work has been featured in *National Geographic Traveler, Time, Outside, Audubon, Outdoor Photographer, Nature Conservancy,* and many others. His images have also been featured in numerous advertising campaigns, books, and calendars around the world.

In addition, Jason also works as one of the leading photography instructors in the country, teaching workshops and classes throughout North America.

To see more of Jason Savage's photography, visit www.jasonsavagephotography.com.